EAT LIKE A LOCAL- NEW YORK CITY

New York Food Guide

Alex Auclair

CZYK Publishing Since 2011.

Eat Like a Local

Lock Haven, PA
All rights reserved.
ISBN: 9798647128829

BOOK DESCRIPTION

Are you excited about planning your next trip? Do you want an edible experience? Would you like some culinary guidance from a local? If you answered yes to any of these questions, then this Eat Like a Local book is for you. Greater Than a Tourist – Eat like a Local, New York City, by Author Alex Auclair offers a local's perspective on some of the best restaurants New York City has to offer.

Culinary tourism is an important aspect of any travel experience. Food has the ability to tell you a story of a destination, its landscapes, and culture on a single plate. Most food guides tell you how to eat like a tourist. Although there is nothing wrong with that, as part of the Eat Like a Local series, this book will give you a food guide from someone who has lived at your next culinary destination.

In these pages, you will discover advice on having a unique edible experience. This book will not tell you exact addresses or hours but instead will give you excitement and knowledge of food and drinks from a local that you may not find in other travel food guides.

Eat like a local. Slow down, stay in one place, and get to know the food, people, and culture. By the time you finish this book, you will be eager and prepared to travel to your next culinary destination.

OUR STORY

Traveling has always been a passion of the creator of the Eat Like a Local book series. During Lisa's travels in Malta, instead of tasting what the city offered, she ate at a large fast-food chain. However, she realized that her traveling experience would have been more fulfilling if she had experienced the best of local cuisines. Most would agree that food is one of the most important aspects of a culture. Through her travels, Lisa learned how much locals had to share with tourists, especially about food. Lisa created the Eat Like a Local book series to help connect people with locals which she discovered is a topic that locals are very passionate about sharing. So please join me and: Eat, drink, and explore like a local.

TABLE OF CONTENTS

DEDICATION

I dedicate this book to my parents. They have supported me in all of my crazy adventures and raised me to be curious and open minded. Without their support I wouldn't have been able to make my dreams a reality.

ABOUT THE AUTHOR

Alex is a high school science teacher in Hell's Kitchen, New York City. He enjoys spending his non-teaching time writing while having a drink at different bars and restaurants around the city. He has lived in New York City for about ten years and has loved every moment of it. In an earlier life he worked as an archaeologist at Mayan sites in Mexico. Traveling and exploring different cultures is in his blood. He is always looking for the next adventure and new dish to try.

HOW TO USE THIS BOOK

The goal of this book is to help culinary travelers either dream or experience different edible experiences by providing opinions from a local. The author has made suggestions based on their own knowledge. Please do your own research before traveling to the area in case the suggested locations are unavailable.

Travel Advisories: As a first step in planning any trip abroad, check the Travel Advisories for your intended destination.
https://travel.state.gov/content/travel/en/traveladvisories/traveladvisories.html

FROM THE PUBLISHER

Traveling can be one of the most important parts of a person's life. The anticipation and memories that you have are some of the best. As a publisher of the *Eat Like a Local*, Greater Than a Tourist, as well as the popular *50 Things to Know* book series, we strive to help you learn about new places, spark your imagination, and inspire you. Wherever you are and whatever you do I wish you safe, fun, and inspiring travel.

Lisa Rusczyk Ed. D.
CZYK Publishing

Greater Than a Tourist – Eat like a Local, New York City, by Alex Auclair offers a local's perspective on some of the best restaurants New York City has to offer.

Alex is a high school science teacher in Hell's Kitchen, New York City. He enjoys spending his non-teaching time writing while having a drink at different bars and restaurants around the city. He has lived in New York City for about ten years and has loved every moment of it. In an earlier life he worked as an archaeologist at Mayan sites in Mexico. Traveling and exploring different cultures is in his blood. He is always looking for the next adventure and new dish to try.

Before becoming a teacher Alex worked as a busser, server, and bartender at different establishments around New York City. He has bartended at biergartens and bars, served at a variety of restaurants, and done both roles at a few Irish Pubs. Working in the restaurant industry has given him unique insight into culinary establishments around the city. You might not like every restaurant you visit in New York City, but he guarantees that the kitchen staff and servers work hard to give you the best experience possible.

When not teaching and writing Alex likes to spend his time outdoors. New York City has beautiful parks. He enjoys walking through the different green spaces around the city with his dog Indiana (yes, she was named after Indiana Jones). When Alex gets out of the city he snowboards around the northeastern United States in the winter and surfs in Rockaway, Queens in the summer. He also plays music whenever possible at local bars or open mics around the city. Alex tries to eat at a new spot whenever possible. It is said that you can eat at a different place, everyday, for your entire life, and still not visit all of the restaurants in New York City. This is not far from the truth, especially since a new spot opens each day.

Now sit back and relax as we explore some of the best restaurants and secrets New York City has to offer.

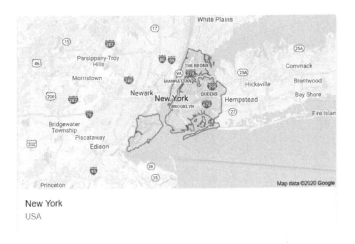

New York
USA

New York Climate

	High	Low
January	39	26
February	43	29
March	52	36
April	64	45
May	72	54
June	80	64
July	84	69
August	84	69
September	76	61
October	64	50
November	55	42
December	44	31

GreaterThanaTourist.com

Temperatures are in Fahrenheit degrees.
Source: NOAA

1. THE BOROUGHS AND GRID

Let's start with the basics. These first few sections will be logistical, but extremely important when traveling and eating in New York City. There are five boroughs that make up New York City. The average visitor spends most of their time in Manhattan, because it's where the main attractions are (think Broadway, Empire State Building, Central Park, etc.). I'll say this now and I promise I'll say it again, use the Google Maps app to get around. It will be invaluable to you on your visit to NYC. Every New Yorker I know uses Google Maps to get to new places, so you will fit right in.

For the most part Manhattan and the other boroughs tend to be laid out in a grid pattern. This means that the city is organized more or less in boxes. For example, if you are on 5th Avenue and you walk to the west, you will come to 6th Avenue. If you continue walking you will come to 7th Avenue and so on. There are exceptions, like there is no 4th Avenue (instead it is called Lexington), but if you are on 3rd Avenue and want to get to 5th Avenue you just have to walk west. Alternatively as you go north the street numbers go up. If you are on 50th Street the next

15

street to your north is 51st Street, and the street to your south is 49th Street. If you are unsure which way you need to walk just follow the numbers, or use Google Maps. Again, Google Maps is invaluable for getting around the city.

2. GETTING AROUND

If you ask me, one of the best parts about living in or visiting New York City is the public transportation. Yes, us New Yorkers love to complain about the MTA (Metropolitan Transit Authority), but if we are honest with ourselves, it makes life so much easier. No need to worry about driving in traffic or losing hours to commuting. The subway allows us to go from the Bronx to Brooklyn, from Manhattan to Queens, you can even take a free ferry to Staten Island (this is a great way to see the Statue of Liberty up close and for free!).

The subway system can be confusing, and the maps are sometimes hard to read if you don't know which way is uptown or downtown. When looking at the subway map put your finger on where you are, then drag that finger to where you want to go. If your finger moves up towards the top of the map you're going uptown. If your finger moves down towards the bottom of the map you're going downtown.

If you're finger moved straight to the left or straight to the right it might be better to just ask either a friendly looking New Yorker or a MTA employee (they will all have uniforms that say MTA on them). New Yorkers get a bad rap for being mean, but most of us aren't so bad and are willing to help you get around.

If the Subway is not for you there are plenty of busses that go around the city. Although, bus routes are slightly more difficult to navigate than the subway because there are so many of them. I recommend downloading the MTA Weekender App (it works on weekdays too), which will help you navigate the public transportation. It includes maps of the bus and subway routes. I am going to say this again because it is so important. If you haven't already downloaded Google Maps do it now. Google Maps will tell you exactly which train or bus to take to get to your destination. It will tell you estimated arrival times and how long each trip will take. It even includes service changes and alternate routes. Please download and use Google Maps, it will make your life so much easier when in New York City.

3. VARIETY OF FOOD IS KEY

One of the greatest things about New York City is the variety of food and cultures. Sure the museums are incredible and the sights are spectacular, but there is nowhere else in the world you can go where you'll find so many different types of food. If you can think of a culture, you can be sure that there's a restaurant in New York City that serves that culture's food. New York City is home to people from all over the world.

Whether you are visiting the city with family or for business there are restaurants for your needs. As you read through the rest of this book keep in mind what foods you really like. Also, think of a type of food you've never had before and would like to try. I promise that whatever food you can think up, you can find it in New York City.

4. PLACES FOR ALL GROUP SIZES.

If you are traveling alone there are plenty of cozy spots around the city where you can get a drink or something to eat. The cafes always have fresh pastries, but if you are a little hungrier I suggest finding a New York Deli and getting yourself a hero (sandwich on a long roll). Katz Deli is famous for their pastrami sandwiches, and don't get me wrong they are delicious, but any New York deli will have excellent sandwiches for you to get a quick bite.

If you are on a romantic getaway for two I would recommend making a reservation somewhere in Hell's Kitchen or Restaurant Row (46th-50th street between 8th and 9th avenue). Any restaurant you eat at in this area will be delicious. In New York City if a restaurant isn't good it'll go out of business in three months. So as you're walking by, just take a glance into a restaurant that looks interesting, if it looks like it's been around for at least three months you're good to go.

For families or larger groups I suggest restaurants where you can get a decent sized table and hear your conversation. Someplace like Carmine's Italian Restaurant or Bareburger (both have multiple locations). Just be careful as New York City is not known for it's cheap meal prices.

5. KIDS

Almost all restaurants are kid friendly in New York City. However, if the establishment is a bar first and restaurant second, they may have a no kids policy. I think New York City is one of the best places to have kids try new things. Sure they may not like a new type of food, but at least you know you gave them the best to try.

There are over 1.1 million kids in New York City. This means we have numerous playgrounds around the five boroughs. There are some really impressive play areas for kids. It may be worth the time to let your children run around one of the larger playgrounds to tire them out or just release some energy. There are several playgrounds in Central Park with everything a kid could want. Also, Union Square has a massive playground in the park. If you go to any park that is close to you, it will most likely have some sort of playground or spot for kids to play.

Broadway always has incredible family friendly shows. But there are also off Broadway shows around midtown and in lower Manhattan. Whether you want to see a Disney extravaganza, or the Blue Man group bang on some trash cans, New York City will have a show for you and the family.

6. WHY VISIT?

I truly believe that New York City is one of the best cities in the world. The diversity alone makes it worth the visit. The architecture is awe inspiring and the parks magnificent, but the food is what puts the icing on the cake. You can literally find any cuisine you can think of in New York City. Not only that, but the dessert shops, cafes, and bars are an experience in and of themselves. When you visit New York City it might make you want to become a local.

7. BEST TIMES TO VISIT

The best time to visit New York City all depends on what you want to do. If you want to see the Christmas tree at Rockefeller center then winter time is when you want to be here. If you want to enjoy New York City parks and all of their beauty, summer time is definitely the time for you.

However, if you're coming here for the food and a good show then any time is a good time! New York City is the city that never sleeps and that goes for the restaurants as well. No matter what time of year, you will find delicious food and good drinks everywhere.

If you do want to come during certain times of year here are some highlights and what you might expect.

Winter - Ice skating rinks around the city, holiday decorations, the Christmas tree at Rockefeller center, holiday markets, snowball fights in central park (just for fun).

Spring - Brooklyn Botanical Gardens, walks on the High Line or across the bridges, outdoor seating at restaurants, beautiful blossoming trees and tulips along walkways, flea markets.

Summer - Surfing (I'm not kidding! Rockaway Beach in Queens has great surfing and a beach town vibe, it's just kind of far away from Manhattan), Coney Island, ferry rides, biking through Central Park, Bronx Zoo (it's free on Wednesdays).

Fall - Pumpkin beer, pumpkin coffee, pumpkin pastries, etc. (we do pumpkin real well here), walking through the parks with sweatshirts and a warm drink, seeing a show (fall isn't our busiest season, so it may be a good time to catch a show when less people are visiting), Halloween is always fun in the city!

8. WHERE TO STAY

Most people who visit New York City stay in Manhattan. There is nothing wrong with this! I would recommend staying away from Time Square as much as possible, because of the huge crowds and expensive prices, but that's just me. Here are my suggestions on neighborhoods to stay in while visiting New York City. They are great areas with many things to do, but will also allow you to access other important destinations.

Recommendations by Borough:

Manhattan - Union Square: This is on 14th Street in the middle of Manhattan. Union Square is walking distance to everything you could ever want in New York City. There are incredible restaurants and bars, as well as, parks, shopping, and street performances.

Brooklyn - Williamsburg: Yes it is full of hipsters. Yes it is expensive. But there is great food and unique experiences (check out Smorgasburg Williamsburg). You'll also find Brooklyn Bowl where you can catch a concert and bowl at the same time!

Queens - Long Island City: This is the first neighborhood in Queens when crossing the East River from Manhattan. Ten years ago this area was practically nothing but warehouses. Now there are hotels, restaurants, and bars everywhere. The best part is that it's only one subway stop outside of Manhattan.

9. CURRENCY TO CARRY

Almost every restaurant, bar, or shop takes credit cards in New York City. However, it is good to carry some United States currency on you. Most street carts don't take credit cards, and you never know when you'll crave a dirty water dog (more on this later).

Also, it is alway nice to tip in cash whenever you get a drink or food.

10. TIPS ON TIPPING

The restaurant and bar industry in New York City is massive. New Yorkers love to eat out and get drinks. But this means that out of the almost 9 million people in the city, many of them work in hospitality. It is important to *always* tip. As a rule you should tip at least 18% on meals. Most New Yorkers tip 20% for a good experience and even more for a great experience. Don't forget, your tip isn't just for your server. It also supports your bartender, food runner, busser, and sometimes the kitchen staff. So please tip generously whenever possible.

At a bar tip 1 dollar for a beer and 2 dollars for an easy cocktail (gin and tonic, rum and coke, vodka soda, etc.). If you are at a cocktail bar and are ordering fancy, difficult to make drinks, maybe leave 3 or more dollars per drink. Being a mixologist is not easy. Especially, if it's done right.

11. HOW FOOD TEACHES US

In New York City you can learn so much about culture just by going to a restaurant. Owners and workers in small family owned restaurants love seeing new faces. They will be more than happy to talk to you about their culture. If you want to learn more about Irish culture, pop into any small Irish Pub you see. I guarantee the bartender will be from Ireland. Or if you want to know more about Italy, France, Turkey, India, the Philippines, Japan, Mexico, Brazil, Ethiopia, South Africa, New Zealand, etc. just find a restaurant in New York City that serves food from one of those countries. The ones I just listed are some of the cultures I've learned about by trying a new restaurant and talking to the people who work there. The best way to learn about culture is to talk with someone from the region over a dish of their traditional cuisine.

People bond over food because we all eat. Everyone has a family recipe or a dish that they love to share. You can learn so much about someone and their culture just by talking about food.

12. STREET FOOD

In New York City there are food vendors on almost every corner. But you can't come to the city and not try one of our famous "dirty water dogs." It will be one of the best hot dogs you've ever had. I highly recommend grabbing a "dirty water dog" (you can just call it a hot dog when ordering) from one of the pushcarts around Central Park, and taking in the excitement and beauty of one of New York City's most iconic green spaces.

If hot dogs are not your thing that's fine too. You'll find food carts and trucks of all varieties around the city. If you pass by a Hallal Guys food cart (keep an eye out for their red and yellow umbrellas) I recommend getting a gyro with the works. Be careful of the hot sauce though, it's really spicy.

Don't be afraid to order food from trucks in New York City. Some of the best tacos and BBQ come from trucks right along the side of the road. Just make sure you have cash, some food trucks and street carts take credit cards now, but not all of them.

13. PIZZA! THE BEST IN THE WORLD!

It is my mission in life to find the best dollar slice pizza in New York City. What is dollar slice pizza you may ask? Let me tell you. It is a slice of pizza for one dollar. Crazy right? Dollar slice pizza is a favorite of starving artists and late night drinkers in New York City. I have been both.

There are countless dollar slice places in New York City. I think some of the best ones are in the East Village near St. Mark's Square (8th street on the East Side of Manhattan). Two Bros has a few different pizza places around the city and all of them have great dollar slices.

Unfortunately, the location of the best dollar slice I've ever had eludes me. I remember having it one late night after a few rounds of drinks with friends. I walked out of the bar and down the block I could see the white illuminated sign with red 99 cent numbers on it. I walked in and had the best dollar slice of my life. The next day when I woke up I couldn't remember where it was! So keep an eye out for the 99 cent sign outside of pizza shops, and you might find the best dollar slice in the city. If you do find it, please get in contact with me and let me know where it is right away! I've been craving it ever since that night.

For people who like to get creative with their pizzas there are plenty of amazing pizza spots around the city. They normally don't have dollar slices, and a slice can cost you as much as five dollars depending where you go. New York City has the best pizza in the world and I stand by that. For some great New York style pizza check out the recommendations below.

Recommendations by Borough:
Manhattan - Prince Street Pizza, located in SoHo (this means South of Houston Street in New York City).
Brooklyn - Joe's Pizza, located in Williamsburg.
Bronx - Yankee J-Z, located in Soundview.
Queens - sLICe Pizza, located in Long Island City.

14. FREE FOOD WITH DRINKS

I'm about to let you in on one of the best kept secrets in New York City. There are bars that give you free food when you buy a drink. You read that right. Free food with a drink. Normally it is the other way around, but not here. I remember when I first moved to New York City I was broke and working in three restaurants to make ends meet. Sometimes I had to choose between drinks with friends or eating dinner, there wasn't enough money for both. But then a bar in the Union Square area of the city saved my life. It is called Crocodile Lounge.

Crocodile Lounge is by far my favorite bar in New York City. It is a dive where you can buy a cheap beer and get a whole personal pizza for free. It is incredible. The pizza is good, the beer is good, it is all good. They also serve any other drink you want, but no matter what drink you order, you get a free pizza. Just please make sure to tip the guys making the pizza, it is hot in the back where the oven is and they are cooking up tons of pizzas.

There are other places that do free food with drinks around New York City. Here are some of my other favorites.

Manhattan - Rudy's in Hell's Kitchen has free hot dogs when you buy a drink.

Brooklyn - Alligator Lounge in Williamsburg is the Brooklyn counterpart to Crocodile Lounge, free pizza with every drink.

Queens - Mad Donkey in Astoria has free peanuts for everyone. The best part is that you *have* to throw your shells on the floor. You get yelled at if you try to make a neat pile on a bar napkin (I know because I've been yelled at). Also, Mad Donkey has some of the best buffalo wings in New York City.

15. COFFEE

New Yorkers love their coffee. You will find coffee shops on almost every corner. We have tons of Starbucks if that is your thing, but I'd recommend going to local coffee shops that are unique to the city. Brooklyn has several coffee shops that roast their own beans and consider making coffee an art. Other coffee shops are a little less serious, but just as delicious. If you are looking for just a quick cup of coffee to drink on the go, keep an eye out for a food cart. In the morning they all sell coffee. Street cart coffee is hot and gets the job done.

If you are looking for some of that fancy coffee check out these places:

Manhattan - Think Coffee, this local chain is found all around downtown Manhattan.

Brooklyn - Partners Coffee, found in Williamsburg, but gets their coffee beans from around the world. Each cup is delicious.

Bronx - Mottley Kitchen, good food, great atmosphere, excellent coffee.

Queens - Sweetleaf, found in Long Island city, their coffee shops always have great hospitality and their coffee is a delicious way to wake up.

16. BRUNCH

There are few things in life that New Yorkers enjoy more than brunch. We love brunch on the weekends. Especially bottomless brunch. What is bottomless brunch you ask? It is brunch that comes with unlimited boozy drinks. Most often these drinks are mimosas, bloody Mary's, or beer. Be very careful though. Before you know it you've had a delicious omelette, six mimosas, and a bloody Mary and it's only 12:30 in the afternoon. It is important to pace yourself, but also have a little fun.

Recommendations for bottomless brunch by borough:

Manhattan - Cuba (a block away from Washington Square Park) you can get unlimited delicious sangrias.

Brooklyn - Randolph Beer WBURG, found in Williamsburg.

Bronx - Charlies Bar & Kitchen, one stop into the Bronx from Manhattan.

Queens - Queen's Comfort, located in Astoria.

17. LUNCH

Oftentimes in New York we find ourselves skipping lunch, or having a really late breakfast. It is a fast paced city, so lunch normally is the quickest meal of the day. That is why we love delis so much. You can hop in, order a delicious sandwich, grab a giant pickle, and hop out. Then you can eat as you walk or sit on a bench and people watch. If you find yourself on Second Avenue stop by 2nd Ave Deli. That is the name of the deli, as well as, its location. It is a traditional New York City Jewish Deli. If you have some time to sit and eat you should definitely try the matzo ball soup or knish. If you have to eat on the run grab a roast beef sandwich to go. You will not be dissapointed.

18. HAPPY HOUR AND ROOFTOPS

Happy hour in New York City normally starts around 4:00 P.M. and goes until 7:00 P.M. The times vary by place, but almost every bar or restaurant in New York City has happy hour. Some are better than others, and some change their specials each day. If you find a spot you like don't be afraid to ask what their happy hour specials are, just so you know for later in your trip. In New York City, the dive bars tend to have the best happy hour specials. If you are on the Upper West Side of Manhattan during happy hour pop into Jake's Dilemma or Gin Mill on 81st Street. They are right across from one another and do buy one get one free drinks for happy hour. Also,

Jake's Dilemma has beer pong tables in the back, in case you are feeling competitive.

If you want to have a drink with a view try one of the rooftop bars in New York City. You can have a cocktail, while taking in the sights. These types of bars can be slightly fancy, so dress as if you were going out for date night. Some suggestions for rooftop bars are.

Recommendations by Borough:

Manhattan - 230 Fifth Rooftop Bar, located right in the middle of Manhattan.

Brooklyn - Westlight, located in Williamsburg.

Queens - Anable Basin Sailing Bar & Grill, although not technically a rooftop bar (it's on a dock) this place has an incredible view of the Manhattan skyline and great drinks and food. It is cash only.

19. DINNER

In New York City everyone eats dinner at a different time. The most difficult times to get a reservation tend to be between 7:00 and 9:00 P.M. Something to keep in mind is that we like to talk, so table turn over at a nice restaurant may be slow. There are drinks before dinner, appetizers, main courses, desserts, and after dinner drinks. Having dinner in the city is a big affair. I have said it before, and I will say it again, if there is someplace you really want to try, you should make a reservation. I enjoy a dinner spot that is a little quieter so that you can have a conversation. If you are into talking to the people you're eating with check out these great quieter dinner spots.

Recommendations by Borough:

Manhattan - Jongro BBQ, found in the Korea Town section of Manhattan. There is nothing like having your meat cooked right in front of you.

Brooklyn - The Meatball Shop, there are a few of these around the city and they are all great. This restaurant allows you to create your own meatball dish.

Bronx - Antonio's Trattoria, found in Little Italy in the Bronx. Most New Yorkers consider the Bronx's Little Italy neighborhood the original one.

Queens - Blend, there are a few of these Latin American restaurants in Queens. There is Blend on the Water (right on the East River), Blend LIC, and

Blend Astoria. They all have similar menus that consist of delicious dishes from Latin America.

20. SEA FOOD

There are many different sea food places around the city. The closer you get to the water, the more you find, which makes sense right? The best fish tacos I've ever had are at Tacoway Beach in Rockaway Queens. That's really far from Manhattan, but if you are here in the summer, and want to check out a New York City beach, it is well worth the trip.

However, if you want a seafood meal you'll never forget, head to The Boil near Washington Square Park. This is a Cajun spot where they serve shellfish (and other seafood) smothered in their house sauce. You can get different versions of the sauce, I'm partial to the spicier one myself, but they are all good. The food comes in a bag full of your choice of seafood covered in sauce. You are given bibs and gloves because it will get messy. It is well worth the mess though. You will finish your bag and want to order more. As of right now this restaurant is cash only, so plan accordingly.

21. SUSHI

For a different seafood feel you can try one of the hundreds of sushi spots around the city. I am a simple sushi kind of person. I like traditional rolls such as salmon rolls or eel and cucumber. But every sushi restaurant has their specialty rolls. If you are looking for a delicious well priced sushi spot, my favorite is Izakaya MEW on 35th Street in Manhattan. The atmosphere, prices, and freshness of the food makes this one of the best sushi spots I've eaten at.

As a side note, every restaurant in New York City is required to display their restaurant's health inspection results in the window. Restaurants that meet all health inspection requirements receive an A. Restaurants that were cited for one or two health code violations receive a B. The letters go down to C and D, but this is rare. After that the restaurant is shut down. One of my favorite take out places in Harlem has a C rating and I'm still alive, so don't count a place out just because of their rating. However, I have a strict only eating at sushi or seafood places with an A rating rule. If you are visiting New York City it is probably safer to just stick with places that have an A rating.

22. BBQ

When you think of BBQ, New York City might not be the first place that comes to mind. But we have some truly delicious BBQ. There are chain restaurants like Dallas BBQ, but I'd stay away from those and eat some local New York City BBQ. If you are looking for a unique experience at a BBQ joint check out Blue Smoke in lower Manhattan. The meat falls off the bone and they have a variety of sauces. The best part is after you're done eating, you can go down to the basement where there is a jazz club. You can continue drinking a cocktail and listen to some great jazz music with a belly full of BBQ.

Sometimes I am hesitant to write about my favorite spots because I don't want them to become too crowded, but I also want you to experience the best. I honestly believe the best BBQ in New York City is John Brown Smokehouse in Long Island City. Food can be pretty subjective, so people might disagree with me, but they'd be wrong. John Browns is a small smokehouse in a slightly industrial area, but their burnt ends are to die for and their chicken is moist and flavorful. They also have live blues music in their backyard and local beer at the bar. I can not stress enough that if you want good BBQ, John Brown Smokehouse is the way to go.

23. EAT LIKE A VEGAN

In recent years there have been a number of new vegan restaurants opening across the city. My favorites are the ones that make vegan burgers that rival real burgers. There is something unique about eating a burger that doesn't have cow in it. If this is your jam too, you definitely need to check out Marty's V Burger on the Lower East Side. It's like eating a burger without the guilt of what the livestock industry is doing to the environment. I am by no means a vegetarian, but I could definitely get on board with eating more vegan burgers that tasted like the ones from Marty's V Burger.

If you are looking for vegan options that are a little more artistic and diverse, try the Blossom restaurants. There are a few around the city and each has a great atmosphere, welcoming staff, and delicious food. Again I am not vegan or even a vegetarian, but there is something special about these vegan spots, and my body always feels much better after eating a meal there. I think it's the all natural plants.

24. BREWERIES

This is the time of the independent microbrewery. For a city like New York, with limited space and millions of people, you might wonder where someone could find enough room to set up an entire brewery to make, can, and sell beer. But in New York there are no shortages of microbrews that create beers.

If you are into the microbrewery scene you probably want to check out some of our more well known breweries such as Other Half (Brooklyn) and Singlecut (Queens). There are other not so well known, but just as intoxicating, breweries across the city. Most breweries serve delicious food to pair with their beers. Take Fifth Hammer in Long Island City for instance. Every day they have a different food truck parked out front of the brewery to make sure you have something to munch on as you enjoy their beer.

Recommendations by Borough:

Manhattan - Torch and Crown Brewing Company is one of the few Manhattan breweries. There aren't many breweries in Manhattan due to limited space and insanely expensive rent.

Brooklyn - Kings County Brewers Collective (KCBC) is right off the Jefferson Street stop on the L train. It is my favorite brewery in New York City.

Bronx - The Bronx Brewery is one stop into the Bronx from Manhattan and worth the trip.

Queens - LIC Beer Project is near all the trains that go into Long Island City. It is a little bit of a walk, but their beer is worth it. Like most breweries in New York City it is dog friendly!

25. BIERGARTEN (NOT TO BE CONFUSED WITH BREWERY)

Biergartens are not breweries. Instead they have large selections of German beer and serve sausages and German dishes. They do not make their own beer, but if you are in the mood for some Oktoberfest style atmosphere and delicious bratwursts then here are some biergartens you should definitely check out.

Recommendations by Borough:

Manhattan - The Standard Biergarten in the West Village

Brooklyn - Radagast Hall and Biergarten in Williamsburg.

Bronx - Bronx Draft House (not really a Biergarten, but great beer and food).

Queens - Bohemian Hall & Beer Garden in Ditmars (last stop on the N and W trains in Queens).

26. BYOB (BRING YOUR OWN BOOZE)

Sometimes you want a cheap bottle of wine to go with dinner. Nothing fancy, just your favorite five dollar bottle. That is okay! No one here will judge you. There are numerous restaurants that have a B.Y.O.B. policy for just such occasions. One of my favorites is a Turkish restaurant on the Upper East Side called Agora. It has phenomenal traditional Turkish food and deserts.

Another B.Y.O.B spot is called Go Nonna in Long Island City (it's just off the Court Square stop in Queens). Go Nonna is an Italian and Argentinian

43

restaurant with homemade pasta dishes and delicious South American cuisine. As of right now neither Go Nonna or Agora has a cork fee (a small fee they add to your bill for bringing your own alcohol), but things do change and many B.Y.O.B. restaurants in the city do have cork fees. If you are unsure if there is a fee just call and ask before heading to the restaurant.

27. ALL YOU CAN EAT!

For those of us who love food and can't get enough, there are special places in New York City just for you. Several different restaurants do all you can eat. This isn't like an all you can eat buffet where you get up with a tray and grab semi warm food from under a heat lamp. These are spots with delicious food that is prepared and brought to you. Every bite is flavorful and every new dish is fresh. If you enjoy meat I highly recommend Fogo de Chão Brazilian Steakhouse in midtown Manhattan. It is some of the best steak and pork I have ever had and it just keeps coming. They have a huge salad bar with delicious seafood, soups, salads, and other accoutrements. The best part is that you have a card with a red and green side. If you flip to the green side, servers will keep

bringing you tender, seasoned meat until you flip
your card to the red side. Be careful because you
might eat so much you won't be able to stand up
afterwards.

There are also many all you can eat sushi places in
the city. Kikoo Sushi in the East Village has great
sushi and sake that keeps coming. Just be aware that
most all you can eat sushi places make you pay for
any sushi you *don't* eat. So start with small orders,
because you can always get more if you are still
hungry.

28. SCREAM FOR ICE CREAM

If you are craving some ice cream on a hot
summer day, or any day, Big Gay Ice Cream has
delicious softserve and all the toppings you could
want. You can find these ice cream shops in the
Lower East and Lower West sides of Manhattan, as
well as, a block off of Central Park on 85th street.

But if you really want to eat your ice cream like a
local New Yorker keep an ear out for the ice cream
truck. They tend to be around parks, but the ice cream

trucks playing classic nursery rhymes can be heard all around the city. I will say this though, the ice cream trucks have good soft serve, but if you want the best you need to find a Mister Softee ice cream truck. Many trucks will have variations of the name Mister Softee, but don't be fooled. The actual Mister Softee is the best. It's like finding a diamond in a bucket of ice.

29. LACTOSE NOT FOR YOU?

If you are lactose intolerant like me, you might take pills or just power through the pain so you can eat some ice cream. Sometimes you just need that dairy in your life. Recently many places have started offering dairy free or vegan ice cream. This is great news for us lactose intolerant people, because we can enjoy all of the deliciousness of ice cream and desserts without the stomach aches. One of the best spots to get a dairy free dessert is Chloe's Soft Serve Fruit Co. in Union Square. Enjoy all the flavors and creaminess with no lactose involved!

Although not technically a dairy free location (or a desert spot), I do need to mention that Bareburger does have the best vegan milkshake I've ever had. I recommend grabbing a unique burger and a vegan milkshake at Barburger for one really good meal.

30. SWEET CRAVINGS

If you have a sweet tooth like me you'll want to know all the best desert places in the city. Unfortunately, there are just too many to list, so here are some highlights. If you're looking for chocolate and you are a *Nailed It* (funny cooking show on Netflix) fan, check out one of Jacque Torres' shops. They can be found in downtown, midtown, and uptown Manhattan.

I love cookies. I could snack on cookies all day and all night. If you have a hankering for cookies then you can satisfy it by going to Insomnia Cookies. These cookie shops are sprinkled throughout the city and always have freshly baked cookies that are gooey and filled with generous helpings of chocolate chips. Insomnia Cookies will keep you up late craving more, and as the name suggests, they are open late to fulfill all of your cookie needs.

One other desert I can't get enough of is cupcakes. Especially cupcakes from Two Little Red Hens on 86th Street and 2nd Avenue. The cupcakes here are always fresh and filled with delicious surprises inside. Take their peanut butter fudge swirl cupcake for instance. Inside you will find the softest, most delicious, peanut butter filling you've ever had. They also have incredible cheesecakes. If you are looking for a New York style slice of cheesecake, then look no further than Two Little Red Hens.

31. KARAOKE

Karaoke is fun. You can't deny that. In New York City there are Karaoke bars all over the place. I suggest spending the night in the East Village and going to one of the Sing Sing Karaoke bars in the area (there are two a few blocks from each other in the St. Mark's area). There's nothing like having a good meal and then topping the night off with some good or badly sung songs. The best part about Sing Sing is that you can rent a whole room for you and your friends or family. You can sing as much as you want and don't have to share the spotlight with anyone else!

32. BARCADE

If Karaoke isn't your thing no worries! There is always something for everyone. Take barcades for instance. These bars serve as arcades where you can drink alcoholic beverages. Is there anything more nostalgic than drinking a beer and playing an old Pac-man machine? I think not. One of the best barcades in the city is in Chelsea. That bar itself is called... Barcade. It makes it easy to find. If you have a roll of quarters laying around it wouldn't hurt to bring it along. You know, just in case you find yourself with some free time during your trip, and you have a hankering for some classic arcade games.

33. PIANO BARS

Sometimes you just want a nice night out listening to some classic sing along songs at a piano bar. New York City is filled with aspiring, successful, and retired actors and musicians. This means that the talent pool in the city is enormous. Nowhere is that more evident than at piano bars. The piano player will take practically any request and you can sing along to your favorite songs. Please make sure to tip the piano player, as it is not easy being a musician in the city.

There are two places that stand out to me when I think piano bar. The first is Don't Tell Mama in Hell's Kitchen. This piano bar gets busy, so you may want to get there early. Buy a drink, sit back, and listen to the incredibly talented musicians at this bar wow you with their skills.

A slightly different piano bar feel is Sid Gold's Request Room. This spot is a mashup of piano bar and karaoke. That's right, you can request and sing your own songs with a real piano player. You will also listen to some incredibly talented singers while you're there. The singers might be well established entertainers, or your average New Yorker with a killer voice.

34. RESERVATIONS

If there is a restaurant you really want to go to, I'd make a reservation. You can either call the restaurant, or most places do online reservations. Just search the restaurant up on Google Maps and the profile there will let you know if they have online reservations. Most restaurants use Open Table for online reservations. If there is someplace that you want to go, then there are most likely other people looking to go there too. It never hurts to make a reservation, plus it helps the restaurant prepare for how many people they will be serving that night. It's a win-win.

35. TAKE OUT

Although I wouldn't recommend take out if you're visiting New York City (it's always better to experience the restaurant scene) it is one of New York City residents favorite things to do. Why not get food from your favorite restaurant without having to get out of your sweatpants or off the couch? If you are visiting I think it is always a better experience to dine in and enjoy the atmosphere of a restaurant. But New York City has made it super easy to get take out if you want.

All you need to do is download either the GrubHub, Seamless, or Caviar app and you will have all of New York City cuisine at your fingertips ready for pick up or delivery.

36. LEFTOVERS

Since practically every New York City restaurant does some form of takeout or delivery there are always to-go containers. Portion sizes vary between restaurants, but you will always be able to take your leftovers with you. Sometimes leftovers are better than the meal itself. I have taken home pizza and eaten it cold, or reheated it the next day. It was just as delicious, if not more delicious, than the night before. Some people don't like cold pizza, I'd argue it is a nutritious and well balanced breakfast.

37. PICNICS

The parks in New York City are beautiful. Even though New York is a city of millions, there are still spaces in parks where you can lay out a blanket and have a picnic. Some of the best places for a picnic are The Great Lawn or Sheep Meadow in central park, and the lawn in Bryant park behind the New York Public Library.

However, some of the more beautiful views, and less crowded parks are outside of Manhattan. Head to Gantry Park in Long Island City or Brooklyn Bridge

Park in Dumbo. Both have large green spaces that are ideal for picnicking and incredible views of the Manhattan skyline.

38. MOVIE NIGHT

If you are in New York City for the summer you should plan on catching a movie in the park. Every night of the week a different park shows a movie on the big screen. You just need to bring a blanket to sit on, some snacks, and your choice of beverages. Then sit back and enjoy the movie. Most of the movies are family friendly classics, so bring the kids along! Or have a romantic date night. Sometimes there is food and drinks available from food carts in the area, but it is always a safe bet to bring your own nurishment just in case.

You can find out which parks are showing movies by checking out the *Time Out New York* website or magazine. Also, the New York City Parks Department webpage has a listing of movies (and free concerts) in the parks.

39. FESTIVALS, FOOD, FAIRS

It seems like there is a new festival every week in New York City. It may help to check out the *Time Out New York* website before visiting to see what is happening while you're here. Each weekend during the summer there are block parties in different parts of the city. During block parties entire blocks are closed to traffic and street vendors set up along the road. You can find delicious foods, fresh produce, and great gifts.

Music festivals are also popular in New York City. You will find festivals like Governors Ball where bands from around the world come to play for an entire weekend. Or there is Electric Zoo if EDM and raves are more your thing. But, you can always find good music any night of the week at jazz clubs or bars around the city. If you're looking for some good Rock n' Roll check out Webster Hall in lower Manhattan.

In terms of food festivals, you definitely don't want to miss the NYC Food Truck Fest if it is happening while you're in town. It features dozens of food trucks and vendors from the area. Only the best of the best are invited, so you can be sure you will have a delicious meal wherever you go.

40. PICTURES TO TAKE

Many people go to the top of Rockefeller Tower or One World Observatory to get pictures from high vantage points. I definitely agree that the views from these locations are beautiful. But they are expensive and full of other people. For great pictures of the city I recommend walking across the Brooklyn Bridge or the 59th street Bridge (also called the Ed Koch Queensboro Bridge). From the bridges you can get spectacular views of the city. Take it one step further and from Brooklyn Bridge park or Gantry Park (found in Long Island City) you will get beautiful views and have an amazing park to walk around in.

Another beautiful walk and picture opportunity is the High Line. It is a repurposed raised railroad track that has been turned into a park. I can't recommend this enough. It is on the west side of Manhattan and runs from Gansevoort Street (you can think of it as around 11th street) to 34th street. There are restaurants under and around the High Line if you get hungry.

I might stop by Artichoke Pizza, which is a favorite of New Yorkers (both the restaurant and the type of pizza). Or if you are here during the summer you should try Frying Pan, where you can eat great food on a retired coast guard boat docked in the Hudson River. Frying Pan is a really delicious and fun way to spend a sunny afternoon. Just be aware that the dock and boat do bounce up and down from time to time. They are in the water after all.

Don't forget if you want pictures of the Statue of Liberty you can always take the Staten Island Ferry for free! There are snacks and drinks on board the ferry as well. You can even create your own booze cruise, as long as you're okay with cheap beer.

41. DRESS CODE

The dress code for the average restaurant is casual, but you will find that in fancier establishments they may require dress shoes, a button up shirt, or a dress. For example, I have been turned away from a few places because I was wearing sandals. Normally it's not a problem, but if you are going out for a fancy dinner or date night, you should probably wear nice c*loth*ing. If you are going for a family dinner or a quick bite to eat, jeans and a t-shirt are always fine.

42. BUYING GROCERIES

If you are buying groceries while staying in New York City you should locate the closest Trader Joe's. Every New Yorker loves Trader Joe's for their reasonable prices and variety of foods. The people who work there are alway pleasant and helpful. Also, if there is a Trader Joe's wine shop nearby you can get bottles of wine for a few dollars. If you ask me Trader Joe's bottles of wine taste just as good as an expensive bottle. I'm not a conoseure, but I do love wine, and I think the cheap bottles at Trader Joe's speak for themselves.

If there is not a Trader Joe's around there should be another grocery store nearby. Although us New Yorkers love to eat out, or order in, we also have to cook for ourselves sometimes. This means that grocery stores are always fully stocked and will have pretty much anything you could need.

43. REMEMBER TO BRING THESE ITEMS WITH YOU

When in New York City I would definitely bring a comfortable pair of shoes. You will be walking more than you are probably used to. I also find a backpack very useful when traveling around the city. Don't forget cash to tip your servers and bartenders.

44. SOLO TRAVELING TIPS

If you're traveling alone and want to meet some new people just sit at any bar in the city and strike up a conversation with the bartender. You can be sure others will join in. For some reason New Yorkers love to talk to other bar patrons. We are fascinated by people. Really, if you ask a New Yorker if they've ever "people watched" (basically just sitting somewhere and watching the people around you) they will say "all the time." People fascinate us. Maybe it is because there are so many in New York City.

Also, when traveling alone make sure to walk around during the day and see what is in the neighborhood you're staying in. There are little hole in the wall restaurants or cafes in every neighborhood. The only way to find these places is to walk around and keep an eye out. It is always exciting to discover a less known, but neighborhoody establishment in New York City. These places tend to have great food and atmosphere.

45. SAFETY TIPS

New York City is a safe place as long as you make good decisions. Since it is the city that never sleeps you will find people out and about at almost every time of day. Bars close at 4:00 A.M. and businesses start opening around 6:00 A.M. so there are always people around. If you are traveling alone make sure to plan out your night. If you are going to be going back to your hotel late maybe take a Yellow cab or Uber. Never get into a car that claims to be a Taxi, but is not bright yellow or green and has the NYC logo on it. You can be overcharged by these vehicles. Feel free to use Uber or Lyft, all New Yorkers do from time to time.

Always carry your wallet in your front pocket because on crowded subways it can be easy for pickpockets to grab things out of back pockets. Also, in subway stations there are blue "call for help" stations where you can contact an MTA employee directly if you feel uncomfortable, or if you have an emergency.

If you need help getting back somewhere ask any police officer or MTA employee (the people who work for the subway or busses). Also, if you get on a bus and feel unsafe for any reason let the driver know and they will drop you off anywhere you need them to along their route, even if it is not an actual bus stop.

New Yorkers look out for one another and they will look out for you. Anyone who works for the city will help if you ask.

46. CONTACTING HELP

When traveling in busy parts of New York City, like Times Square, you will see police officers on duty almost everywhere. They are always willing to help in any way they can. Also, any MTA employee will help you if you need directions getting somewhere. If you are uncomfortable for some reason don't be afraid to reach out to a city employee. If it is an absolute emergency dial 9-1-1 and emergency services will be sent to you.

47. APPS AND SOCIAL MEDIA

As I discussed earlier, Google Maps will be invaluable to you. It will tell you what trains or busses to take. It will also plan walking or biking routes for you. I think this is the most important app to have downloaded before visiting New York City. I also believe you should follow *Time Out New York* on all social media, as this magazine always has free and new things to try even for us New Yorkers.

48. WHAT TO READ

New Yorker's most trusted newspaper is, of course, the *New York Times*. This paper is read all over the world, but while you're here it might not be a bad idea to pick up an issue. You'll know that your issue was created not too far from where you're standing.

When it comes to magazines the Holy Grail for New Yorkers is *Time Out New York*. This magazine is published on Wednesdays and includes everything you'd need to know for your upcoming weekend. It has listings for free shows, great restaurants, and new bars. You can also find funny articles and stories from local New Yorkers. Every issue has helpful information about what is happening in the coming week, and where you can check out your favorite musicians, comedians, and artists.

You can find *Time Out* outside of most of the main subway stations. Just look for the bright red *Time Out* distribution bins, or for people handing out the magazines wearing *Time Out* shirts. Make sure to read the featured restaurants and bars sections. They always have great suggestions.

49. MANNERS

Something to keep in mind about New Yorkers is that we are honest and loud. This may come across as rude and abrasive, but normally it's just the way we talk. If you grew up and spent most of your time in a loud city you'd always be shouting too. New Yorkers will tell you as it is. If you are in someone's way they might say excuse me loudly or seem harsh. They are not trying to be offensive, they are just trying to get where they are going. In New York try not to take things personally, we are just loud people.

50. AMOUNT OF TIME NEEDED

You will never be able to see all of New York City in one trip, and you should not try to. I have lived in New York City for almost ten years and I am always finding new things to do. I'd recommend no less than five days in the city. In those five days I would try to limit travel to one, maybe two boroughs. You do not want to spend all of your time on the Subway, and I promise you are going to stumble upon interesting restaurants and fun things to do just by walking around.

There are so many parts to New York City that you will want to come back again, and that's okay. Try to plan on doing one or two things a day and then just give yourself free time to wander around.

BONUS TIP 1: MUSEUMS

I don't know where to begin. I love museums. New York City has some of the most incredible museums in the world. I would have to first recommend the American Museum of Natural History. Between the dinosaur skeletons, and amazing planetarium shows, you could get lost in this museum for a whole day. Each hall is full of science and facts that will teach people of all ages something new. Plus, Central Park is right next to the American Museum of Natural History and there are restaurants lining the streets just outside the museum. Fun fact, if you're a Tom Hanks or Meg Ryan fan, Cafe Lalo from You've Got Mail is only a couple blocks away. I've eaten the pastries there and they are delicious!

If science isn't quite your thing another recommendation would be the Metropolitan Museum of Art, nicknamed The Met. This museum is directly across the park from the American Museum of Natural History and is full of art from around the world. You can see mummies from ancient Egypt or sculptures from Rome. There are paintings from artists you know well, and masterpieces from artists you may never have heard of. If you are in New York

City during the warmer months then here is a secret. There is a cafe on the roof of The Met that not many people know about. You can get a snack, coffee, or some wine and gaze across Central Park as you enjoy your food and drink. It is absolutely beautiful, and since the museum does not advertise the cafe is up there, it's rarely busy.

There are so many museums in New York City that I could write an entire book just about why you should go to each one. But let's talk about a museum that I think is underrated and doesn't get nearly as many visitors as it should. The New York Transit Museum is in Downtown Brooklyn and it is so much fun. You can walk through and sit in train cars that go back over a hundred years. There is so much to learn about the massive system of tubes and railways that crisscross New York City. If you find yourself in Brooklyn, and you have some time, you should definitely check out the New York Transit Museum.

BONUS TIP 2: PLACES TO SHOP

If you are looking for high end shopping New York City has what you need. If you walk along Fifth Avenue in Midtown you will find every boutique and brand name you can think of. Also, you will find high end shops around Rockefeller Center and along Lexington Avenue. There is definitely no shortage of shopping in the Big Apple.

In Time Square you can find souvenir shops everywhere. If you need to pick up gifts for people back home, you can buy all the knick knacks and souvenirs gifts you could ever want in Time Square.

If you are looking to shop a little more local, and have a unique experience, you should check out the markets that pop up from time to time around the city. During the holiday season there are holiday markets in Bryant Park and Union Square. Also, keep an eye out for street fairs that close down entire city blocks to sell food and crafts.

BONUS TIP 3: LEARN SOME PHRASES

New Yorkers talk like everyone else in the United States, we just might have a different accent or change our vowels to an aw sound. Think water (w-aw-ter), or dog (dawg), or coffee (c-aw-ffee). But here are some phrases that are unique to New Yorkers:

Bodega - a corner store or deli.

Hero - a long sandwich, sometimes called a sub.

Watch the Gap - be careful of the hole between the platform of the train and the train itself.

The City - when someone in New York says "The City" they are referring to Manhattan only, even though there are four other boroughs in New York City.

Uptown/Downtown - Remember if you are going north it is uptown and if you are going south it is downtown.

READ OTHER BOOKS BY CZYK PUBLISHING

Greater Than a Tourist- St. Croix US Birgin Islands USA: 50 Travel Tips from a Local by Tracy Birdsall

Greater Than a Tourist- Toulouse France: 50 Travel Tips from a Local by Alix Barnaud

Children's Book: *Charlie the Cavalier Travels the World* by Lisa Rusczyk

Eat Like a Local

Follow *Eat Like a Local on* Amazon.
Join our mailing list for new books
http://bit.ly/EatLikeaLocalbooks

Eat Like a Local

Printed in Great Britain
by Amazon

13582672R00048